EMMA'S STORY

Emma's Story

SHEILA
HOCKEN

Illustrated by Janet Kerr

LONDON
VICTOR GOLLANCZ LTD
1981

Text © Sheila Hocken 1981
Illustrations © Janet Kerr 1981

ISBN 0 575 02890 4

*To my daughter Kerensa
in the hope that she will read
and enjoy this book*

Photoset in Great Britain by
Rowland Phototypesetting Limited, Bury St Edmunds, Suffolk
Printed by St Edmundsbury Press, Bury St Edmunds, Suffolk

Contents

Chapter 1

Leaving Home

My name is Emma and I'm a chocolate coloured labrador. Most other labradors are black or yellow, but not only am I a very special colour, I was a very special dog. I say "I was" because I'm fifteen now. If I were human I'd be a hundred and five, and at a hundred and five nobody still works, do they? But I used to be a guide dog—and that isn't something any dog can do. So I'm going to tell you how I became a guide dog, right from the beginning, from when I was a puppy.

I was picked out of my litter. My brothers and sisters were black, and I was the only chocolate one. Perhaps that's why I was chosen. I remember, when I was about six weeks old a strange lady came to the house and stood and watched us playing. She smelt very nice—she smelt of other labradors. You can always smell what breed a dog is. Of course, we dogs have extra special noses, not like you human beings. You must miss an awful lot in life not being able to smell all the exciting things . . . Where was I? Oh yes, I was the only one who ran up to smell round her feet, and she had some very exciting stringy things in her shoes which I decided would be nice to play with.

"I like this one," she said to our owner. "What's her name?"

"Emma."

"I think I'll take her. I hope she'll make a guide dog. I think she will, she looks just the sort of puppy we're after."

"You're a regular puppy walker, aren't you?" said our owner. "I've seen you in the town. What do you look for in a guide dog?"

"Well . . . steadiness, friendliness. She doesn't seem at all frightened of strangers, she seems keen to meet people, bold. I'll clap my hands and see what she does."

I looked up at the banging noise and rushed over to her again to make another fuss. She was attracting my attention.

"That's one of the most important things. She mustn't be afraid of noises."

At that point she picked me up and fondled me.

"Oh you are lovely, Emma. Would you like to be a guide dog?"

Of course, I didn't know what she meant then. I'd never heard of guide dogs. It wasn't the sort of thing my brothers and sisters talked about. All we were really interested in was playing and when the next meal was coming along.

"I'm sure you would,' she continued. "Yes, I think I'll take this one."

"When will we know if she's trained as a guide dog?" our owner asked.

"Well, it will take about a year to puppy-walk her, and then she goes to a Guide Dogs for the Blind Association Training Centre for a further five or six months of intensive

training. I'll let you know how she's getting on."

This strange lady started to carry me out of the house, away from the rest of the puppies. I didn't think I was going to like that and I started to call back to them, "Hey, she's taking me away. Help me!"

"There, there, Emma," she said. "Don't worry."

Of course, she didn't understand what I was shouting. She took no notice of my screams as we walked up the garden path. Then we got into a peculiar thing and she sat down and put me on a seat beside her. I was so startled I stopped shouting. It didn't smell very good—sort of, well, a thick smell about it. I didn't trust it at all.

"There, Emma, now we won't be long. You sit quietly while I drive."

There was suddenly a tremendous noise and we started to move. I could see trees and houses going past us. That was horrifying. I jumped off the seat straight away and tried to hide in a corner on the floor. Although it was dark under the seat, it was still very noisy. I couldn't get away from that terrible noise, but at last it stopped and I was picked up and whirled down another garden path and into a house, and into a room I knew was the kitchen. Kitchens always smell beautifully of food.

No sooner had my feet touched the kitchen floor than I saw a huge yellow labrador coming towards me. I can tell you, I was frightened. I didn't know whether she was going to be friendly or not so I flattened myself to the floor and closed my eyes tightly in the hope she wouldn't see me. I could feel her sniffing round my ears.

"Hmmm, so you're the new puppy she's been talking about, are you? You're a funny colour."

I couldn't resist saying something. "I'm chocolate," I squeaked. "I'm a chocolate labrador."

"Never heard of them. Labradors are always yellow or black. Chocolate indeed!"

"Now, Miranda, this is our new puppy. Her name's Emma," my new owner said. "Isn't she beautiful?"

"Huh!" Miranda snorted. "I don't know about that. You might have bought one the same colour as me." But, of course, our owner didn't hear her.

"Now you will look after her, Miranda, won't you? You'll be a good foster mum for her."

I wasn't so sure. I daren't move, I was still glued to the floor. I must admit, I couldn't resist opening my eyes and

having a quick look round, even though I was terrified.

"Oh well, I suppose we'll have to get on if you're here to stay, for a little time at least. You won't be here much longer than a year, I hope," Miranda said.

I didn't like that. What did she mean? I wasn't going to be here much longer than a year? I'd only just been dragged away from my brothers and sisters and now she was talking about me going somewhere else. But I didn't ask. She didn't look like the sort of labrador you could ask questions.

"There's the bed over there," she instructed.

I looked over into the corner. Well, it looked a nice enough bed. It was big, with lots of blankets.

"We both sleep in there and you have to learn to be houseclean, too."

"What do you mean?" I asked. "Houseclean?"

"What I mean is, you go out into the garden when you want to do anything."

"Oh!" I didn't really know what she meant but I was sure I was going to learn fast with her around. No sooner had she said that than my new owner scooped me up and rushed me out into the back garden.

"There's a good girl, Emma. Busy girl, Emma, busy girl."

There were lots of interesting smells on the lawn, and leaves all over it—lots of different coloured leaves, yellows and reds and browns.

"Aren't these lovely?" I said to Miranda. "Where do they all come from?"

"They fall off the trees. It is autumn, you know."

"Autumn!" I said. "What does that mean?"

"It's the time of year. It comes every year and all the

leaves drop off the trees."

"How marvellous!" And I started to chase them as they magically floated up in front of me in the wind. Diving at them. Tearing at them. Well, even if Miranda wouldn't play, the leaves were good enough for me. When I was fed up playing with those, I had a sort round the garden. There were loads of bushes, flowers, daisies. It was a marvellously interesting place to be, everything was so beautiful. I'd never noticed it was autumn before, and I'd never seen so much grass. All the blades were different colours. A lovely sweet, damp smell hung about the air. Life was so good.

No sooner had things got really interesting out there than I was whipped up again and taken back into the kitchen. Miranda was sitting in the middle of the floor looking huge and menacing.

"It'll be teatime soon, pup, and you'll get yours and don't try and take any of mine either, or else." She lifted her lip and I saw all her teeth and they were big. I knew, however hungry I was, I wouldn't dare pinch any of Miranda's dinner.

"Now, sit quietly while Paddy gets our dinner or she gets annoyed."

"Paddy?" I said.

"Yes, that's her name. We all call her Paddy. It's so much easier than saying 'Owner' or 'Mistress'."

"Paddy," I repeated. "Yes, that's an easy name to say."

"No rushing round her ankles," Miranda snapped at me, as I started towards Paddy when I saw her getting dog bowls out and putting food into them. "She won't stand for that, so you might as well learn straight away."

I sat back again. Ooh, it smelt so beautiful, I wished she'd hurry up. I tried whining a bit to hurry her up. Miranda gave another snap. "And none of that noise around here. We don't have badly behaved dogs in this kitchen, so shut up."

I had to sit back patiently and quietly and wait till my bowl was put on the floor before me. As soon as we'd finished our meal, Miranda led the way to the garden again. She looked back to make sure I was coming.

"Come on then pup, Paddy always expects us to have a walk round the garden before bedtime."

I followed. Whatever she did I would do, and then I couldn't go far wrong. I followed her round the lawn, round the paths and the flower gardens, and back into the kitchen.

"Come on you two," Paddy called, "you can come in the lounge for a while, while I listen to the radio."

I followed Miranda out of the kitchen door, through the hall and into another big room that was carpeted. Lovely soft carpet on the floor. Beautiful. I rolled in it, it was so comfortable. Then I spotted the fire. A big blazing fire in the corner. It was interesting to watch—the flames danced and darted and burned yellow and red. I had just got settled in front of it when Miranda poked me with her nose.

"Move, pup. I get first seat near the fire. You go back there."

"But it's so warm, let me stay here."

"Do as you're told," she snapped. "That's my place. You get behind me. Anyway, you mustn't get your nose all dried up with those flames."

"I won't do that," I promised, trying to get her to let me stay there.

"Move out of the way," she growled again.

I hadn't got much choice. After all, she was much bigger than I was. It wasn't too bad, even if I was behind Miranda. I could put my head on her back and watch the flames.

I must have dozed off for an hour or two, then Paddy started calling us into the kitchen and into the big bed in the corner.

"Good night, Miranda. Good night, little Emma. Be a good girl. You've got Miranda to keep you nice and warm." She leant over the bed and stroked my head, and off she went and closed the door behind her. Miranda and I were alone. I was a bit frightened. I wanted to talk but I was afraid whatever I said would be the wrong thing. I tried to think of something that wouldn't upset her.

"What's it like living here?" I asked, eventually.

"It's very nice. Especially if you behave yourself," she added, with a stern look in her eye. "No chewing and no stealing food are the basic rules to remember. You can't go far wrong. Always do as you are told, especially by me."

"Well, what do you do all day?" I asked, thinking of my brothers and sisters I had left at home. We had found so much to do together, there were so many games to play in a day.

"What do you mean, what do I do? I do plenty around here. Don't be cheeky."

"Oh, I didn't mean to be cheeky, I just meant . . . well . . . there's nobody to play with, is there?"

"That's not the only thing you do in life, you know.

You've got a lot to learn if you're going to be a guide dog."

"Oh yes, I heard them mention guide dog. Well, what does that mean?"

"You'll learn. You're not old enough yet. I'll tell you some other time when you get a bit older and you've got a bit more sense. Now go to sleep and stop asking so many questions."

I closed my eyes but I felt cold and lonely in the corner of the bed. I began to think about my mother and my brothers and sisters. We'd all be curled up together, putting our heads on one another, and mother would be there to watch over us. It was so safe at night. Now I felt afraid. I looked over at Miranda in the other side of the bed. She'd gone to sleep already. I plucked all my courage up and crept over to her for warmth. If I closed my eyes I could pretend that she was my mother. In no time at all I must have fallen fast asleep.

Chapter 2

First Lessons

"Good morning, Emma. Good morning, Miranda. Come on then, off you go out into the garden," Paddy called.

Miranda leapt off the bed and greeted Paddy.

"There's a good girl, what a clever dog, Miranda."

So that was the thing to do when you saw a human being! I followed her and started to jump round Paddy's feet and bite her slippers. They were lovely furry things.

"Emma, don't do that! Go on, into the garden."

We were hustled out. Miranda rushed round the lawn and I rushed after her. I tried to get her to play. I made a snap once or twice at her tail but she wasn't having any of that. She went to sit at the back door.

"Come on," I said, being very brave, "let's have a game."

"Don't be silly. Sit quietly, it's nearly breakfast time. She'll let us in soon, and after breakfast we shall probably go out."

"Out! Out where?"

"Oh, I don't know. We go out different places every day. Ah, here she comes. Go on."

We went into the kitchen and after breakfast, sure enough, Paddy came along with collars and leads. I'd never seen a collar or a lead before and when she started putting the collar around my neck, well, I wasn't very keen. It felt stiff and hard. I tried to back out of it but it seemed to hang on and get even tighter. I couldn't scratch it off.

"Oooh, I don't like this," I shouted at Miranda. "Tell her to get it off."

"Behave yourself, Emma. That's your collar. You can't go out without a collar," Miranda snapped at me.

"Come on, Emma." Paddy bent down and stroked me. "It won't hurt you, you'll soon get used to it." And then she clipped the lead on to the collar and started to drag me out of the kitchen. "Emma, come on, there's a good girl. We're just going into the garden today. Come along."

It was horrible, especially being dragged along the floor. Then Paddy produced a toy out of her pocket and started squeaking it. I forgot all about the collar and lead and dashed forward to catch it. Every time I just got my teeth near it, she moved it away. Still, it was an exciting game and we played for ages on the lawn. It wasn't until I got tired and sat down that I realised I had still got the collar on. Goodness, I thought, I must have got used to it already. Oh well, it's not so bad if when they put your collar on it means they're going to play.

After dinner we went out on the lawn again. Miranda and Paddy. Collar on again. I looked for the squeaky toy but it didn't appear this time, so I sat down.

"Come on, Emma. Come on, lead. Good girl."

What did she mean, "lead"? She started to pat her leg. I got up—maybe there was something interesting there—and I ran over to have a sniff. Paddy kept saying, "Lead, Emma. There's a good girl." She picked leaves up off the lawn and started to throw them in front of me. Well, this

was another marvellous game. I ran off in front of her. "There's a good girl. Lead, Emma," she kept repeating.

"Emma, sit!" Paddy suddenly said, and pushed my bottom down onto the floor. "Sit!" she repeated. "There's a good girl." I looked round at Miranda who was lying over on the other side of the lawn, watching.

"What's all this for?" I said.

"You have to learn to be obedient," Miranda said. "'Sit' means sit down. 'Down' means lie down. It's very easy when you know all the commands. All you have to do is do it when they ask you."

"Can't we play?"

"You can't play all the time. I told you that last night. You have to learn to be obedient first."

Paddy started tugging the lead again. "Lead, Emma. Lead, Emma. Good girl."

I ran forward. At least it was interesting. We were walking round the lawn together and she was talking, telling me lots of nice things. Suddenly she stopped and pushed me down again. "Sit, Emma. There's a good girl."

I remembered next time she stopped, and when she said "Sit" I sat down.

"Oh you are a clever girl, Emma. You're certainly going to make a guide dog if you learn so quickly. Tomorrow I'll take you out into town—get you used to all the traffic, see what you think of that."

That night in bed I asked Miranda, "What's town?"

"Town's the place where all the people go. All the cars and the buses and lorries and shops and all sorts of things are in town."

"What are lorries . . . and shops?" I asked.

"Oh dear, you don't know anything, do you, puppy. Didn't your mother teach you anything at all?"

"Well, she never mentioned lorries."

"Lorries are great big things, like cars, only much, much bigger."

"A car was the thing I came in, was it?"

"Yes, that's right. Humans use them all the time, they never think of walking. They get in those things to go wherever they want to."

"And what are shops?"

"Oh, I wish you weren't so inquisitive," Miranda growled.

"What does inquisitive mean?"

"Goodness me, will you never stop asking questions? That's what inquisitive means. I shall get no sleep if you don't shut up."

So I closed my eyes and off I went to sleep, but not until I'd thought about shops, and lorries, and cars, and lots of people. What was it all about? I was soon to find out.

The next morning, on went the collar again and the lead, and we set out down the front path, to the pavement. Every time we got to a step where a road was, I had to sit down.

"There's a good girl," Paddy said. "You have to sit at all the kerbs and wait for the cars to go by."

I didn't really understand this but I soon got the hang of sitting at every kerb. Miranda did it, so I just followed suit. We started getting into a much busier area. Lots of cars along the road. Hundreds of people along the pavement. It amazed me how they all got around without walking into each other. There seemed to be so many legs to cope with. I was lucky I'd got Paddy and Miranda to follow. At least they knew where they were going.

"There's a shop," Miranda said suddenly.

I looked up. People were coming and going in and out of a doorway and there were lots of things displayed in the window. I had a sniff.

21

"Mmmm, that smells nice," I said. "Foodish, but not meat, is it?"

"No, that's a cake shop and you don't have cakes, you're a dog. Only humans eat those."

"Why don't we have them?"

"Because cakes and sweets are bad for our teeth. Now then, along here there are lots more shops and you'll probably have to learn the names of them, so stop asking questions and listen to Paddy."

"Here we are, Emma. This is the cake shop," Paddy said. She stopped and pointed to the doorway, then went on. "This is the Post Office. You must remember these Emma, so you learn which shop is which."

I was very mystified. I couldn't understand why I should have to know the names of the shops if she knew them already. As we turned the next corner I flattened myself to the ground. There was such a noise, such a terrible banging and crashing, that it seemed to be taking me over, and the pavement trembled beneath me.

"Come on, Emma. It won't hurt you."

"What is it, Miranda?" I squeaked.

"Oh, they're only drilling the road, they're always doing that. They make such an awful lot of noise about it but they don't actually do us any harm. Come on, you're expected to walk past that without batting an eyelid."

"Come on, Emma," Paddy encouraged, stroking me. "It won't hurt you."

She could see that I was terribly frightened and she picked me up and walked nearer the noise. I tried to bury myself under her coat but she wouldn't let me. She put me back down on the pavement and stood there.

"There we are, Emma. It's very noisy but it won't hurt you. Look, it's only a road drill."

Eventually, I did get used to the noise and I wasn't so frightened. I sat up to have a look. Curiosity got the better of me. There were lots of men digging holes in the road and making a mess around the place. Well, it was true, they didn't seem to wish me any harm. After a while, I got quite bored with watching them so I just walked past, wanting to know what else we were going to do that day.

"With a bit of luck," Miranda whispered to me, "we'll go to the butcher's. Now that is a very important shop because Paddy gets all our meat from there, and if we're both very good, we might get a bone. But there's no jumping up at the counter, no barking, and unless you sit perfectly still inside the shop the butcher will be annoyed."

I followed Miranda and Paddy meekly into the shop, afraid to make a wrong move because if I ruined the chance of getting a bone, I knew life with Miranda wouldn't be worth living. I sat quietly while Paddy ordered things over the counter.

The butcher suddenly spotted me. "Oh, what a nice puppy," he said, "and so well behaved. I think they deserve a bone each. There we are, I'll put some in with your order."

"Thank you very much. They'll be delighted with those."

As we walked out of the shop Miranda said, "Good girl. You did behave yourself. We both got a bone. Well, you're learning fast, aren't you, young lady? Maybe you will be a guide dog after all."

Chapter 3

Christmas Eve

I soon forgot all about my brothers and sisters and my mum because life with Paddy and Miranda was so exciting. We went out every day to different places. Into the shops; alongside road-works that I never even looked at any more—I knew what they were, so they didn't bother me; by big lorries and cars. I got used to it all.

"We're going Christmas shopping today," Paddy said, as she put our collars and leads on one morning.

"What's Christmas shopping?" I asked Miranda.

"It comes round once a year—Christmas that is—and there's plenty of preparation for it, believe you me. I should think it will be really packed in town today. Everybody will be out, bustling to get to the counters and into the shops. It'll be dreadful, mark my words."

As soon as we got out of the front door my nose began to tingle. It was so cold. Then I noticed the garden looked different.

"Frost!" Miranda announced. "As if we won't have enough problems in town today without this."

"Frost! What's that?"

"Frost? It's that stuff all over. Can't you see it? Can't you feel it?"

I looked about again. It was dazzling. The sun was shining on the trees, and the leaves, instead of being green, were coated with some sort of glittering, shiny stuff. The lawn had got it on as well. The paths and the pavements were slippery. I had a hard job keeping on my feet, even though I'd got four.

"Put your feet down carefully," Miranda shouted at me. "Don't try to run like that, you'll slip all over the place."

I tried placing my feet carefully. Every time one of my paws touched the pavement I slipped, so I had to keep trotting to stick with Miranda and Paddy. "I don't think I like this very much," I gasped to Miranda. "Does it come often?"

"Not too much. It comes in winter."

"What's winter?"

"You do ask a lot of questions. Winter comes between autumn and spring. We get snow as well."

"Snow? That sounds exciting. What happens then?"

"You wait and see. You'll have a big surprise."

As we approached the shops, we met crowds of people.

"There's a lot of people out, Miranda. What are they all doing?"

"I told you, they're Christmas shopping. It will get worse as we get into the shops."

It was very difficult to keep up with Miranda and Paddy. The worst thing was sitting at the kerbs. Every time I sat down, somebody stepped on my tail.

"You'll have to remember to tuck your tail underneath you," Paddy told me. "You might have to work in a really busy city. It's a good idea for you to get used to crowds."

As we went around the next corner into the main shopping street I was stopped dead in my tracks by a sight I'd never seen before—a huge tree in the middle of the road, lit up.

"Goodness me! What in the world is that, Miranda?"

"It's a Christmas tree."

"A Christmas tree! It's got lights all over it, what are they for?"

"Oh, you know these humans. They always like to decorate things. Well, that's what they do at Christmas. They get trees and put lights on them and all sorts of other things as well."

"Yes, but what's it for? What does it do?"

"It isn't for anything," Miranda said, impatiently. "It doesn't do anything. Now shut up, it won't hurt you."

"But what is Christmas all about? If they have trees with lights on, what else do they do?"

"There's Christmas Day, of course. Now that is nice," she said. "We get presents. Everybody gives everybody presents on Christmas Day."

"Ooh, what do we get?"

"Well now, let me see. We might get a bit of turkey. We might even get some squeaky toys and probably big chew bars."

It was the thought of Christmas Day that kept me going through the town that day. We got hustled and bustled and trodden on. It was enough to make even the best dog nasty tempered. I was only too glad to get home and rest. I was absolutely exhausted. I climbed into my bed and nearly fell fast asleep. I say "nearly" because Paddy was in the kitchen doing lots of cooking. What lovely smells were coming from that oven! Tired as I was, I just had to stop awake to see what was happening.

"She's making mince pies," Miranda informed me, "and sausage rolls, for Christmas."

"Ooh, lovely," I said.

"It's all right you saying lovely. We don't get them."

"Don't we get anything?"

"We get lots of toys but we don't get mince pies and sausage rolls."

Paddy took the pastries out of the oven and left them to cool on the draining board, and off she went. I got out of bed, following my nose to the drainer.

"Oh, the smell is so mouthwatering," I said.

"You mustn't touch them," Miranda told me. "That is a terrible sin. You must never touch food unless it's given to you in your bowl."

But I was deaf to Miranda's warnings. The smell was too great for me to resist. If I could stand up on my hind legs and just give a little leap, I could get that mince pie that was almost on the edge . . . I made it. Oh, the taste! Still-warm mince pies are delicious! I looked up again but I couldn't reach any more—she had pushed them too far back.

"If she finds out—"

Suddenly, Paddy came back into the kitchen before Miranda had time to finish her sentence. No sooner had she got in the door than she looked at me. "Emma, you bad, bad dog! You naughty dog!" She came over and smacked my nose. I was horrified. I crept into the corner of the bed and tried to hide under the blankets. "You are a naughty dog,

Emma, you must never do that again."

"How did she know I'd pinched it?" I asked Miranda when Paddy had gone.

"You've got pastry crumbs round your whiskers. If you're going to steal, you might at least hide all the evidence and lick your face clean."

It was Christmas Eve. There's something very special in the air on Christmas Eve. Not a smell, just a feeling—although there are lots of nice smells too. Those mince pies again, sausage rolls, and a delicious smell coming from the oven that Miranda informed me was turkey.

"We'll probably get some tomorrow, being Christmas Day. We're bound to have a treat. Of course, you won't be here next year, so you'd better make the most of it now."

That upset me a bit. I wished she wouldn't keep telling me that I wouldn't be there next year.

There were lots of different sounds in the air as well with people coming and going. I heard everyone who came say, "How's your new puppy, do you think she'll make a guide dog?" Paddy always invited them into the kitchen to come and say hello. That was delightful.

"I think she's coming on well," Paddy would tell them. "She seems to learn very quickly, although come the New Year I think her serious training will begin, how really to be a guide dog, and I must teach her lots of different things about leading and finding shops and how to find empty seats on buses and things like that," she explained.

"Do you train her to guide?" one visitor asked.

"Well no, not exactly," Paddy said. "You see, I'm a puppy walker. We have to give puppies the grounding.

29

They can't go out to be guide dogs when they're puppies, obviously, so they have to learn how to live in the house as a pet. Every guide dog is going to be a pet, after all, and live as a pet does in a household. So they have to get used to all the comings and goings. They have to go round the shops, on and off buses, trains. All sorts of things they need to learn. So I don't actually put Emma on the harness—they'll teach her that when she gets to the Training Centre—I just teach her to walk in front of me and to sit at the kerbs, to obey commands like 'Sit' and 'Stay' and 'Come'."

"That's fascinating," the visitor said. "You are a clever puppy, Emma. Aren't you a good girl?"

It was lovely. They made such a fuss of me. They hardly said a word to Miranda. I felt very important, especially when the carol singers came round. It was early evening and I could hear children singing outside. I started to bark. Miranda leant over and snapped at me.

"Stop barking, you silly thing. It's carol singers, you don't bark at them."

"I'll try and remember for when Christmas comes again," I said meekly.

Paddy went to the door and I heard her talking.

"Well, really, we've come to see Emma as well as sing you carols," the children were saying.

They all crowded into the kitchen. "She's going to be a guide dog," I heard them say. "That one, the chocolate one."

"Isn't she a beautiful colour?" another one said.

They all came round to pat me and fondle me. It was so exciting. I wished Christmas Eve would come more often

30

than once a year. After they'd all gone, Paddy started to get ready to go out. We knew she was going out—the smell of perfume. She only put that on when she went out and you could smell it all over the house. She came back down and Miranda rushed to greet her.

"Miranda, I'm sorry, I can't take you with me. I'm going out to deliver Christmas presents. Oh, all right." She gave in, Miranda dashing round her. "Perhaps I can take you with me if you're a good girl, and I'm sure you will be."

I jumped up. "Take me as well," I said, "please take me. I'd love to come Christmas present delivering."

"Emma, get down, you'll get your paws all over my dress. Now go and be a good girl and get in your bed. We won't be long."

"Miranda, don't go without me. You're going to leave me on my own!"

"You can't come out. You're only a puppy. Go back to bed and go to sleep, we won't be long."

"Oh no, please don't go. I've never been on my own before."

"Well, you'll have to learn. You're bound to get left on your own when you get older so the sooner you start the better." She disappeared round the kitchen door without another word.

I heard the front door bang and the car start. It was no good crying, I thought, there was nobody here to listen. I padded round the kitchen and tried the bed. It seemed so big and empty without Miranda. She wasn't terribly friendly, but at least she was another dog I could talk to. Then I noticed the kitchen door. They hadn't closed it

properly. I managed to get my nose round and pull it open. Oh, the lounge. How lovely—it wasn't so bad being left on my own if I could go in there. Lovely warm carpet on the floor, and the fire to lie in front of. Suddenly I noticed one of those Christmas trees in the corner. I didn't know we had one in here and I went up to have a look. It had shiny balls hanging from it. I could see my face in some. I banged one with my paw and it fell off and rolled on the carpet. I started to push it with my nose and then made a dive for it. It shattered all over the place. That wasn't very good. I tried another one. It was easy getting them off the bottom branches but they smashed every time I pounced on them. I couldn't reach any more, they were all too far up the tree. Oh well, the fire was still blazing, so I lay down and went to sleep in front of it.

I heard the front door open and sat up to greet Paddy and Miranda. But, as Paddy came in the door, she looked horrified.

"Oh Emma! What have you done? Look at the mess. My Christmas tree. You bad dog."

She seized me and I was dragged into the kitchen and smacked and the door slammed behind me. I crept into the bed next to Miranda.

"What have you been doing? Honestly, we can't go out for ten minutes and leave you alone. What have you done in there?"

"I was only playing with the Christmas tree."

"Playing with the Christmas tree! What did you do with it?"

"There were some things on it, you know, like balls, but every time I started to play with them on the carpet, they broke into pieces and went all over the place. I didn't do anything else."

"You didn't do anything else! Don't you think that's enough? Oh dear. Well, that's your turkey gone tomorrow. You won't get any."

"Oh Miranda, will you give me some of yours?"

"I most certainly will not. Go to sleep. Get away from me, you are a naughty dog."

It was hours before I went to sleep. I was so upset about the whole business. I wish I'd never seen that Christmas tree. But Paddy did forgive me because she gave me some turkey on Christmas Day, a squeaky toy and a rubber bone. I had a marvellous time, playing in the garden most of the day.

Chapter 4

Snow

I hate rain, especially when it's cold and windy with it. I don't even have to go out and have a look to see if it's raining. I know, the moment I wake up. I can smell it.

"We won't go out today, will we Miranda?" I asked.

"Well, of course. We always go out, rain, wind, hail or snow. Paddy goes out every day, you ought to know that by now."

"But I'll get wet," I said.

"So what! You've got a waterproof coat, haven't you?"

I had to admit that I had. Labradors do have waterproof coats. They have what you might call two coats. If you were to brush the fur the wrong way on my back, you'd see my top fur is long and coarse and underneath I have a very close, soft coat, a little lighter in colour. A sort of milk chocolate. But that doesn't save me getting my paws wet and it gets wet under my tum as well—I haven't got a double coat there. Apart from that, although the top coat doesn't actually let the water through, it holds it and it gets heavy and horrible.

"Come on, you two," I heard Paddy call from the front door. Miranda rushed through the kitchen into the hall. "Where's Emma?" Paddy asked Miranda. Paddy looked round the door. "Come on, Emma, we're going out."

"No thanks," I said, burying my nose under the blankets.

"Emma, come on. Don't you want to go for a walk?"

It was no good protesting, I knew she wouldn't understand. She put my collar on. I plodded slowly to the front door and noticed Paddy had got wellington boots on, rain mac and umbrella. She wasn't going to get wet even if we were. We went out, down the path and on to the pavement. It was flooded. There were puddles everywhere. Miranda splashed through them regardless.

"How could you?" I said. "Look, you are getting me even wetter."

"It's lovely walking through puddles," Miranda said. "Labradors are water dogs. I suppose it's because you're a chocolate labrador that you're odd. That's probably why you don't like water. Anyway, I should think it'll turn to snow soon. It's very cold." She put her nose up into the air and sniffed deeply. "Yes, I can smell it coming."

I sniffed. "I can't smell anything," I said, "except horrible rain."

"Can't you detect that note of real coldness in the air?"

"Detect!" I repeated. "What do you mean?"

"Can't you smell something different about it?"

"Well . . . maybe," I said, not wishing to appear stupid, "but I've never smelt snow before, have I? What's it like?"

"Oh, you wait and see. If you don't like rain, I don't know whether you are going to like snow."

We got to the first kerb. "Sit, Emma," Paddy commanded.

"Not likely," I said. "In that great puddle there?" I started to back off.

"Come on, Emma. You must sit at the kerb regardless of the rain."

I saw a car coming up the road and went back a bit further. I knew what was going to happen, even if those two didn't. I got well hidden behind Paddy's boots when . . . whoosh . . . and those two got soaking wet. After they'd shaken themselves down a bit I crept out. Paddy looked down at me and started laughing. "You're not stupid, are you Emma? You could see what was going to happen. You are going to make a good guide dog if you have got that sort of intelligence."

Intelligence? I thought, it's just common sense to get out of the way if a car is coming and you know it is going to splash you.

We crossed the road into town. I had to jump over all the puddles because Paddy and Miranda seemed to wade straight through them. It was bad enough getting wet through, without having to traipse through puddles as well.

"I think we'll just go to the pet shop this morning," Paddy said. "It's a bit nasty to go round much. See if you can find the pet shop for us this morning, Emma. You come round here, Miranda, stay at the back of me. Lead, Emma, straight on."

I knew what she meant by now. "Lead" meant I had to walk a few paces in front of her and she'd taught me to walk down the middle of the pavement. I knew where the pet shop was and I didn't need any encouragement to get there. I took her straight in, up the step and through the door, and sat at the counter. Next to the butcher's, it was my favourite shop. Paddy ordered our biscuits and some chew bars—as we wouldn't be able to play much in the garden, she thought I might get bored in the afternoon. So on we went home again, thank goodness.

The other thing about getting wet, apart from the horribleness of it, was that we weren't allowed in the lounge when Paddy listened to the radio or watched television. We had to get dried off first and it took ages, even though Paddy rubbed us with towels. My coat seemed to hold the wet on the outside for hours and hours. Of course, I had to go in the garden every now and again to attend to the calls of nature. So, on the whole, I felt a rainy day was a miserable wasted day, even though we did get the chew bars, which passed an hour or two.

In bed that night, Miranda woke up and started to poke me with her nose.

I jumped. "What's the matter, what's the matter?"

"It's snowing," she said. "Look out of the window."

I looked and instead of being really dark, as it always was out there, it seemed much lighter. White. I could see white spots passing the window.

"Gosh, is that snow?" I said. "Yes, I can smell it now. I know what you mean. Well, what is it, Miranda?"

"Actually, it's rain, just frozen, but it's so totally different that I never associate it with rain. There aren't any puddles or anything like that to go through."

"Thank goodness for that," I said "What happens outside?" I ran to the window and tried to jump up but I couldn't reach. The only things I could see were tops of trees. Well, I thought they must have been tops of trees—

they didn't really look like them any more, because the leaves had gone and the branches were just snow white.

"Snow white," I said to Miranda. "Now I know what the saying means. Isn't it beautiful?"

"You wait till the morning comes and you see the back garden. You won't recognise it at all. You won't be able to find the paths or the steps and the grass will be buried."

I could hardly sleep, waiting for morning. I was so excited. When Paddy came into the kitchen I was first at the back door waiting to go out.

"Off you go, Emma. See what you think of that snow."

I stood there, almost blinded by the brilliance of it. It was so white. Everything sparkling, beautiful white. I had to

shut my eyes for a minute to get used to it and open them again. It still dazzled me so I screwed my eyes up before I went out into the garden. Immediately my feet were freezing. I picked them up one by one and shook the cold stuff off.

"Ugh! Oh, I don't know about this, Miranda, it's clinging to me."

"Run about a bit, that will get you nice and warm. You'll forget about it then."

I ran forward and slipped down the steps. "Ooohh!"

"I told you to remember the steps, didn't I? I said you wouldn't see them in the snow."

I looked behind me and saw my pawprints. "Isn't that clever?" I moved forward a bit and looked round again. "Miranda, where's the lawn gone?" I said in dismay.

"It's still there," Miranda pointed out. "It's under that snow."

I was getting the idea of it now. It wasn't too bad if you picked your feet up and jumped more like a kangaroo than a dog. So I started to leap round the lawn. This really was fun, especially all the tracks I'd left. Miranda started to jump about as well. I was amazed. I'd never seen her enjoying herself so much. I put my nose down into it to see what happened. It was cold—but what fun! I pushed my nose right along through the snow and made a big trench, all piled up at the sides. Paddy came out with gloves and coat on, and started to pick up pieces of snow and throw them for us. That was a great game! The only thing was that by the time I got where she'd thrown it, it had disappeared. Then there were the bushes. I found if I went to a bush and

nudged it, all the snow fell off. It was marvellous, I could clear every bush. I rushed round the garden shaking them with my nose or my paw. That amused Paddy so I did it all the more.

Miranda seemed to have a new lease of life. She was like a puppy again. We played Tag round the lawn, chased each other round the bushes. By the time we'd finished that morning there wasn't one shred of snow left on a bush anywhere. Then I had to find my way back to the house for lunch, but I followed my tracks up the steps. I could tell where they were this time. I wouldn't be fooled again, I thought, I'd be careful next time I came out.

By the time we'd had lunch and a nap in bed and Paddy opened the door again for us late in the afternoon, the snow was beginning to change. It was grey looking. There were patches of lawn showing through, and I could see the steps quite clearly now. I put my foot out onto the ground outside.

"Ooooh, this is sort of rain and snow mixed."

"Yes, it's melting," Miranda announced. "That's the trouble with it. It looks so nice while it's here but once it goes like this—slush, they call it—it's quite dreadful. I wouldn't stop out long if I were you." Miranda dashed out after me, and quickly returned to the kitchen.

Chapter 5

A Visit to the Vet

The next day, when it was time for us to go out, Paddy decided we wouldn't go very far. The slush had frozen, and the pavements were like sheets of ice.

"I think we'll just go round to the park this morning," Paddy said. "It should be easier there, there'll be grass to walk on and it won't be so slippery."

In the park, a totally different picture met my eyes. Usually we just met a few odd dogs there, maybe a person or two, but this morning it was filled with children with sledges—so Miranda informed me—and those without were making slides on steep grassy slopes. They were sliding down on their feet and sometimes on their bottoms. The sledges came whizzing down the other slope. You have to be careful about children. You never know what they're going to do next. They run around screaming, throwing things at each other, and if you get in the middle they'll throw them at you as well. I was longing to have a go on the slide, I must admit, but having to brave dozens of children to do so, I thought twice about it. It wasn't until most of them had gone that I dared have a go. I rushed up the slope to the top and before I had hardly got my two front paws on the slide I was down at the bottom again.

"This is great!" I shouted to Miranda. "Come on, have a go."

"No thank you. You might do yourself some damage doing that. I'd stop it if I were you. Dogs have been known to break legs on slides."

But I would not listen to Miranda. She was an old stuffy. I kept rushing up to the top and sliding down, especially as Paddy stood at the bottom and laughed at me every time. Then, somehow, the next run I got my paws in a ravel and something went wrong because when I got to the bottom, I was in agony. I lay in the snow, crying. "Oh, Miranda, help me. My paw, I've done something to my paw."

Paddy came rushing over. "Emma, what have you done? Let me have a look."

I held my paw out for her.

"Oh dear, poor Emma, can you walk?"

I stood up but I held the hurting paw high so it wouldn't touch the ground. It was throbbing now. Miranda sauntered over.

"I told you so, didn't I? You'll have to go to the vet's now."

That didn't sound very nice, especially the way Miranda said it. "Vet's, what's that?"

"You have to go there when you're sick. He'll make you better but it's very unpleasant. That'll teach you to do as I tell you in future, won't it?"

Paddy picked me up and carried me home. After making a telephone call, she got the car out of the garage and lifted me onto the back seat.

"Now don't move, Emma. I don't know what you've

done with that leg so lie down and be a good girl. We'll soon have you at the vet's."

That word. It sounded awful. Sent shivers down my spine. Paddy carried me out and into a different house. I didn't like the smell at all—disinfectant—and we sat in a room with lots of other dogs and cats. I daren't say anything to any of the other dogs. Nobody was saying anything at all. They all sat there looking terrified. I began to shiver. There was obviously something very, very wrong with this place.

"Don't worry, Emma," Paddy said. "There's a good girl. The vet's a nice man, he'll soon have you better."

It was our turn to go in, so we moved out of the waiting room into another room. Paddy placed me on a table.

"Hello, is this your new puppy?"

"Well, I've had her some months now," Paddy told him, "but, touch wood, I've never had anything wrong with her till today."

"What's she been doing?" the vet asked.

"Silly dog, she's been sliding in the park. Must have done something to her front paw."

The vet came towards me and held my paw. He had a feel and a prod. I tried to pull my paw back.

"There's a good girl, don't be frightened. What did you say her name was?"

"Emma," Paddy told him.

"There's a good girl, Emma." He felt round a bit more. "Hmm, I think she's pulled a tendon on this joint." He pointed to the joint where my paw bent. "We shall have to put a bandage on that for a few days, young lady, and no vigorous exercise for you."

He started to bandage my paw. I didn't like that. I couldn't bend it when he'd finished, and I felt very restricted. I must admit, though, it did ease the pain in it a bit. Paddy carried me out, back to the car, and home we went. I was put straight to bed in the kitchen.

"Poor Emma," Paddy told Miranda. "You won't have to let her chase round. You must be very nice to her while her paw's getting better. We won't be able to go out till she can have the bandage off."

Miranda got into bed beside me. "Now look what you've done. You've stopped our walks. I shan't get out until you're better."

"I'm sorry, Miranda, I didn't realise what would happen."

"Well I told you, didn't I?"

"Yes."

"Perhaps you'll listen to me next time. Remember, I'm much older than you are and much wiser."

By the time my paw was better, all the snow and the ice had gone. There was still a chill in the air but at least the pavements were dry. We went off into town to do the usual round of shops. Then Paddy told us that this morning we'd go to a cafe for a cup of tea.

"You've never been to a cafe before, Emma. It's about time you learned how to sit under a table and how to behave yourself where there's lots of food about."

That sounded interesting—food.

"It's this way, turn left up here, Emma."

Off I went, leading the way.

"Find the cafe, Emma. Find the cafe," Paddy repeated.

Food, I thought, I'll smell out a food shop and, sure enough, I did.

"That's a clever girl, this is the cafe," Paddy said.

In we went. There was lots of clattering of cups and the air in there was lovely and warm and steamy from tea and the smell of fresh baked bread. We got to a table and Paddy drew the chairs out.

"Under you go, Miranda. You follow, Emma."

Miranda got under the table and lay down. I sat there, smelling the air.

"You behave yourself in a cafe," Miranda whispered. "No trying to get food off tables. If anybody offers you anything you must ignore them."

I watched as a young girl came across and brought Paddy a cup of tea and something on a plate.

"That looks nice, Mavis," Paddy remarked. "Have you just made them?"

"Yes, we've just done a fresh batch of doughnuts. They're very good. I've tried one myself."

Mavis looked under the table. "Is this your new puppy you're walking to be a guide dog? I've heard a lot about her. Emma, you call her, don't you?"

She smelt lovely. I licked her hands as she put them out to stroke me. Mmm, sugar, it was delicious.

"She's chocolate!" Mavis said suddenly. "Is she a labrador?"

"Of course I am," I said.

"Yes," Paddy said. "She's a pedigree labrador. There aren't many chocolates about, you know."

"Oh, she is lovely. Can I fetch them something to eat?"

"No, please don't," Paddy said. "You see, if Emma's going to be a guide dog, she's going to have to learn that when she takes her owner into restaurants or cafes she can't have any food, so that she'll sit under the table and behave herself. If I start giving her titbits here and now, well, you can imagine what'll happen when she gets a blind owner, can't you? She'd make a nuisance of herself begging from people, trying to get scraps off the floor and so on."

"Yes, of course. I never thought of that. She is beautiful." She gave me one last stroke and off she went.

"Don't we get anything?" I asked Miranda. "Nothing at all?"

"No," she said shortly.

I could see some crumbs under the next table and tried to edge my way over. As the lead tightened Paddy told me to "Leave".

"No, Emma. Come back." She pulled the lead.

I thought, I'll sit here for a moment till she thinks I'm being good, then if I make one quick grab I can get that big crust that somebody's dropped. I sat for a minute or so—it seemed hours—while I was watching that crust. Yes, she was eating her doughnut, she wouldn't be holding on tight to my lead. I lunged. I got it. And then something dropped on me from above. I'd somehow got my lead round the table leg when I moved and Paddy's cup of tea dropped all over my head. Ugh, it was awful—hot and sticky. I couldn't get it off.

"Emma! You bad girl," Paddy said. "Now look what you've done, you've got my cup of tea all over you and the floor. They won't let me bring you in here again."

I'd have to remember in future that if I dived for crusts I got soaked with horrible sticky, hot tea. I didn't think I'd do it again. I sat quietly under the table while Mavis came and mopped up and gave my head a wipe as well. She was very nice.

"I am sorry," Paddy explained, "but she is only a puppy and she's got to learn all these things."

"That doesn't matter. It's only a drop of tea on the floor," Mavis said. "It'll be all right. Look, I've cleaned it up and given Emma a wipe as well. I think maybe you ought to bring her in more often, don't you? Get her used to it, and maybe we could put a few crusts round and teach her that she shouldn't take them."

"Yes, that's a good idea," Paddy agreed. "Labradors are terrible for food, you know, they eat anything. Anybody would think I didn't feed them properly."

Mavis laughed. "They look well enough fed to me."

I daren't move from under the table until Paddy said that we were going home again, then I crept out very quietly to the door, looking round to make sure no one would notice me. I felt they were all talking about how stupid I was, but nobody seemed to be looking, so I shot out the door quickly, back onto the pavement. It was chilly outside after that lovely warm cafe. We went there about twice a week after that and I never ever touched another thing on the floor. As long as I live, I shall remember how embarrassing it was to have a cup of tea on my head.

Chapter 6

The Training Centre

Paddy came into the kitchen very early one morning. She seemed to be in a hurry.

"What's happening?" I asked Miranda. "Are we going somewhere special today?"

"I'm going on holiday," she announced.

"What do you mean *you're* going on holiday. What about me?"

"You're going to the Guide Dog Training Centre."

"Why can't I come on holiday with you?"

"Because you're going to be a guide dog. I go on holidays. Perhaps you'll come later on in the year when we go on the big holiday, but this time you will have to stay at the guide dog kennels."

"What does it mean, being a guide dog?" I asked.

"You'll find out soon enough."

"Why can't you tell me about it? You must know, you're always telling me how much older and wiser you are than me."

"Don't be cheeky," she snapped.

"I'm sorry. I didn't mean to be cheeky, but you are always saying that and you do know everything, Miranda."

She snorted down her nose and walked over to make a fuss of Paddy and pretended I wasn't there. When we got into the back of the car I was determined to ask her again.

"Why aren't you a guide dog, Miranda?" I asked, as soon as Paddy started up the car. "Aren't you clever enough?"

She dashed across the seat and bit my ear. She was very angry. I had obviously said the wrong thing.

"Don't you ever say that to me again. Of course I'm clever enough to be a guide dog. Somebody has to stop at home with Paddy to help train the puppies she has."

I was so afraid of her, I sat right up in my corner and didn't dare say anything else for the whole of that long journey. Miranda never even said goodbye when I got out of the car at the kennels.

"Come on, Emma, you'll really enjoy your weekend here. There're lots of other dogs to talk to and you'll get to know what it's like in guide dog kennels," Paddy said.

I jumped out of the car and was met immediately by a young girl.

"Hello Emma, I haven't seen you before. Oh, you really are a nice chocolate labrador, aren't you?"

At least she knew what I was, I thought. She had obviously been told about me.

"Bye, Paddy, hope you have a nice time. I'll see you on Monday. Don't you worry about Emma, we'll look after her."

"Bye, Chris." Paddy got back into the car.

Chris led me down a path and into a long corridor. So these were kennels, I thought. Well, they didn't look too bad. I glanced in the gates as I passed. Little rooms. There were all sorts of dogs there. The young girl stopped.

"Here you are, Emma. Go and meet your kennel-mate.

I'm sure you'll get on with him fine. We'll go out for a walk later on."

She pushed the gate open and left me there in the kennel. There was a big bed in the corner with a big yellow labrador on it. I thought Miranda was big but he was three times her size. In fact, honestly, if I hadn't smelt labrador about him, I'd have really believed he was a donkey. I was a bit frightened so I just sat in the corner and looked at him.

"Hi there, my name's Anton," he announced, jumping off the bed and rushing towards me. He was obviously friendly.

"I'm Emma."

"You come to stay?" he asked.

"Just for a couple of days, I think. Paddy has gone on holiday."

"Who's Paddy?"

"She's my owner."

"Ah, yes, well I've been in here since yesterday. It's not bad at all. We go out for walks and there are lots of other dogs to talk to. Food's good, too."

"I'm pleased about that," I said.

"You're going to be a guide dog, are you?" Anton said.

"Well, yes, I think so. That's what everybody tells me. What do you know about guide dogs, are you going to be one?"

"Oh yes, I am," Anton announced proudly.

"What does it mean?"

"I'm not really sure. You'll have to ask the dog next door. He's a Wales collie—I think that's what he said he was. Sort of shaggy and brown and white. Not a labrador-type at all, but quite a decent chap. I was talking to him this morning in the run. He seems to know quite a bit about it. He's been in once or twice before."

"That's interesting. When will we meet him?"

"When we've had tea we usually go out in the run. I don't think that'll be long now."

Sure enough, after tea, we were out in the run and I saw the big brown and white shaggy dog next door.

"Excuse me, Wales collie," I said.

He cocked an ear but never turned. "Ehm, Wales collie!" I called, a bit louder.

He looked round. "Are you talking to me?"

"Er, yes. I wonder if you could help me?"

"What did you call me?" he said.

"Wales collie . . . aren't you?"

"I'm a Welsh collie. Goodness me, where have you been brought up?"

"I'm awfully sorry," I said. "Welsh collie. Do you come from Wales?"

"Well, I suppose you could say that, originally."

"Is it a long way away?" I asked.

"Why, I don't know. I've never been there."

"I thought you said you had."

"No, I said I was a Welsh collie. What are you?"

"I'm a labrador, a chocolate labrador," I hastened to add.

"Have you been to Labrador?"

"Oh no."

"Well then, why do you expect me to have been to Wales, just because I'm a Welsh collie? Now what did you want?"

"I wanted to ask you about being a guide dog," I said.

"What does it mean?"

"Well, it means that we come in here—when we're quali-fied of course, and you are obviously too young yet—then we're trained to be guide dogs and we go out with new people to take them about."

"Why do we have to take them about?" I asked.

"Well . . . I'm not really sure," he admitted, "but we are being trained for it and they will tell us when we get to the Training Centre proper. It's up the road, you see," he said. "This is just a place for dogs like us, puppies you know, who are being puppy-walked."

"I do wish I could find somebody who'd tell me about being a guide dog," I said. "It's so infuriating. I'm having to learn all these things and I don't really know why. I know it's a very special job and everybody thinks I'm wonderful but I wish they'd tell me a bit more about it."

Another dog was let into the run.

"Goodness me! Look at her ears, Anton. What's the matter with them?" I said.

"Hush, she'll hear you. There's nothing the matter with them, she's an alsatian. They all stick up like that."

"Phew, I bet they get cold."

"Excuse me, but I'm not an alsatian. Well . . . I am . . ."

I wish she'd make up her mind, I thought. Maybe with ears like that it was difficult.

"Really I'm a German shepherd dog. My name's Sugar."

"Hi, I'm Anton."

"And I'm Emma. I'm a chocolate labrador."

"You're unusual. Well, as I was saying, I'm a German shepherd dog. We've been called alsatians for so many years, but it's wrong. We were originally bred to herd sheep in Germany. All the rest of the world calls us German shepherd dogs but the English people call us alsatians. We're having a movement to try and correct it and ask them to use our proper title."

"Why is it that English people call you alsatians?" I asked.

"Well, many years ago, apparently, there was a war between England and Germany, and English people didn't want any dogs they thought had come from there, so instead of calling us German Shepherds they called us alsatians."

"What's a war?"

"It's when people fight."

"Fight!" I said in amazement. "I thought only dogs fought."

"Huh, you'd be surprised," the Welsh collie said, "people are worse than dogs."

"That's very interesting," I said to Sugar. "If I ever meet anybody who's interested in your breed, I'll pass it on."

"Thank you. I'd be grateful if you would."

She seemed such a nice dog, I thought I'd ask her. "Are you going to be a guide dog?"

"Oh yes," she said.

"Do you know what it's all about?"

"Yes, I do know a little about it. I have a friend who's a guide dog."

"Oooh, really." I felt very excited. "Go on, tell us all about it."

"I haven't known her very long. We meet on our walks every morning when I go out shopping. She wears a white

harness and she has an owner who can't see. That's why we're being trained to stop at kerbs and find shops. I assume you two are being trained the same as me."

We both nodded.

"Apparently, these people are blind so they ask us if we wouldn't mind taking them to their place of work, onto buses, to shops, all that sort of thing."

"It sounds rather complicated," I said. "Do you think we'll be able to do all that?"

"I'm sure I will." Sugar seemed to have great confidence in herself.

"What's it like to be blind?" I asked her. "Do you know?"

"Yes, the guide dog down the road told me. Shut your eyes."

I did, briefly.

"No, keep them shut," she said.

"Now what do I do? It's all dark in here and I can't see anything."

"Exactly. Well that's how it is to be blind, but all the time."

I opened my eyes in utter astonishment. "You mean it's like having your eyes closed?"

"Yes."

"Oh, how awful."

"Of course, having guide dogs makes life much better for them," Sugar told me.

"Yes, but how do they cook and how do they plant things in the garden?" I thought of all the things Paddy did every day.

"Apparently they are very good. They always find ways

round difficulties and a lot of them go out to work. My guide dog friend says that all the blind people she knows are very nice and, of course, being guide dogs makes us extra special. We do a really good job of work you see, so they are very grateful to us."

I realised then how important my training was and that I'd really have to concentrate on what Paddy was telling me if I was going to be a guide dog, and now I was sure I really wanted to be one. I'd have to work hard when I got back home.

To be perfectly honest with you, I forgot all about Miranda until bedtime came and, even then, it wasn't bad because I'd got Anton to curl up with and he was much more friendly than Miranda. We chatted long into the night about where he lived—somewhere in Birmingham, he told me.

"How old are you?" I asked him.

"I'm six months. How old are you?"

"Gosh! I'm six months, but you're a lot bigger than I am."

"Oh yes, but I am a male you know. We always grow bigger than females, and perhaps it's because you're chocolate that you're small. I wouldn't worry about it. I don't think it makes that much difference what size we are, do you? As long as we're going to be guide dogs in the end."

The next two days at the Guide Dog Centre were so packed with interesting things to do, I hardly thought about Paddy and Miranda. We went out for walks, but all together—I mean, me and Anton and the Welsh collie and Sugar. We had lots of time to play on the fields. We didn't do any training. The meals came regularly and they were very tasty. The beds were comfortable, and it was lovely and warm. They're the sort of things that a dog thinks about, whether she's warm and well fed. The girls there were so kind to us—we got brushed every day, just like we did at home. In fact, it was quite a surprise when Paddy turned up on the Monday to take me back home again. I jumped in the car. Miranda sat there on the back seat.

"I've had a lovely time," I said to Miranda. "It's been marvellous. I met Anton, a Welsh collie, and a German shepherd dog called Sugar."

"German shepherd dog!" Miranda snorted. "Never heard of them. You must have got it all wrong. You probably mean a sheepdog or a Border collie."

"No I don't, I mean a German shepherd dog. You probably know them as alsatians, but that's the wrong name."

Miranda turned to look at me. "I've met a lot of alsatians, what do you mean it's the wrong name?"

I explained about German shepherd dogs being called alsatians in this country because of a war between England and Germany, just as Sugar had told me.

"Never heard such rubbish in my life. I don't know what they're teaching you at that Training Centre, I'm sure." She turned away and stuck her nose out of the window.

"Well, I had a marvellous time there. I bet you would have enjoyed it, Miranda."

She just snorted and continued looking out of the window.

"It was so interesting talking to Anton. He's like you but a lot bigger, being a male. Males are bigger you know." I thought I'd show off and talk about a few of the things I'd learned while I was at the Training Centre. "And the Welsh collie was fascinating to talk to. And, of course, Sugar told me all about being a guide dog."

"Oh yes," Miranda mumbled.

"She has a friend who's a working guide dog. They wear a white harness."

"Really," Miranda said, shortly.

"Have you had a good time? Where did you go? What did you do?" I remembered to be polite and ask her.

"We've been to the seaside and I had a marvellous time. We stopped in a very nice hotel, carpets on the floor, you know. And lots of sand. I went swimming in the sea."

"What's the sea?"

"It's a great big expanse of water and it moves. Oh, it's so exciting to go in it—but of course, you won't be going for a long time. We won't go on holiday until the summer, now."

"Do you think I can go with you then? Although, I don't know, I might like to go back to the guide dog kennel. It was so interesting."

"You'll probably come with us on the big holiday. You'll have to learn all about travelling on trains and going to the seaside and stopping in hotels. There's a lot to do before we go. After all, you haven't even been in a restaurant yet, have you?"

"No," I said.

"Or a train. You've never been in a train."

"No. I've never heard of them," I said. "What are trains and restaurants?"

"You'll learn. I'm so fed up of explaining what things are. I had such a lovely weekend, nobody to keep badgering me with silly questions. It's been so peaceful."

"Yes, I've had a lovely time too," I said. I decided that if she could be funny with me, then I would be funny with her, and I turned to look out of the window and didn't say anything else until we reached home. After all, I was getting quite grown-up now and it was about time Miranda stopped bossing me about. Anton had taught me that. He said it doesn't matter how old you are, if you're going to be a guide dog you're much more important than any other dog and I wasn't to forget it.

Chapter 7

Spring Digging

The day after we arrived home Paddy said, "It's almost springtime and there's so much to do in the garden. We'll just have to stop in today, Miranda and Emma. You can help me. I think we'll weed first and then we'll put all the new bulbs in."

It was lovely helping Paddy in the garden. Digging up weeds—I gave her a helping paw there—watching her put things in. It was very interesting. I noticed she buried lots of different things in lots of different places. I went round after her and I could still smell where they were. I could smell her scent on them, even though she'd buried them in the ground.

After lunch Paddy said she'd put in everything she wanted to, and was now going to do some baking in the kitchen, but as it was quite sunny I could stop out in the garden. I went round again sniffing all the things she'd buried. Perhaps she'd left them there and wanted to get them out again later, like I did sometimes with bones? If I did that for her now it would save her such a lot of time.

So I went round and dug them all up. They were little round things and I decided I'd place them outside the back door as a special surprise for her when she'd finished baking. It took me ages. There were about a hundred. I might have missed one or two but I kept going round the garden to check that I'd got as many as possible. I sat down when I'd finished in front of my pile of bulbs. Won't she be pleased, I thought, when she knows I found every one and brought them all back for her?

It wasn't long before she opened the door.

"Emma, come on in, it's teatime."

Then she spotted the bulbs. I sat there looking pleased with myself. "Look what I've done," I told her. "I've dug them all up for you. I could smell where you'd put every one."

She suddenly started laughing. "Oh Emma . . . no. What have you done? You've dug all my bulbs up. They were going to be flowers in the spring. Oh, Emma!"

I knew she wasn't annoyed at me because she kept on laughing. But what did she mean, "they were going to be flowers"? She'd buried them in the garden. She wanted to save them, didn't she? Well, there they were in a big pile. I'd found every one. Wasn't she pleased?

"Oh dear, Emma. It's going to take me a whole afternoon to plant them again. I'll have to do it tomorrow. You musn't dig them up, not when I've done it again."

I couldn't understand it. I went up to her and wagged my tail. I knew she couldn't understand what I was telling her so I tried to explain. "But I've brought them all back for you," I repeated. I ran up to the pile and fetched one and gave it to her.

"Yes, Emma. You're a very clever dog, but they really ought to have stayed in the ground."

So we spent the whole of the next day putting them all

back again. Paddy made sure she didn't leave me in the garden after that. She made me come in and sit in the kitchen.

"Now Emma, you musn't go and dig the garden up, or we won't have any flowers in the spring or the summer. They must stay there to grow. I know you thought that you were doing a good turn but you weren't really. You'll have to learn not to dig in the garden."

Miranda sat on the bed as usual, with one of those smiles on her face. "You silly dog," she said, when Paddy had gone. "You dug every one of those bulbs up, did you? I heard her telling you off."

"Well, she didn't exactly tell me off," I said. "In fact, she was laughing about it, so it must have been funny. Although I didn't think it ought to be funny. I mean, I'd brought them all back for her. I thought she'd have been delighted. I thought I'd saved her such a lot of time finding them again. I knew exactly where they were. Paddy would never have found them again, would she?"

"Tut, they come out and flower," Miranda explained. "You don't have to find them again, you leave them there so that they can grow. You'll see them coming up soon, the green shoots and then the flowers coming out. They make the garden look very beautiful."

Chapter 8

The City

"We're going to the city this morning, so we'll have to find the bus stop, Emma. Now you must learn how to find bus stops. Here it is, along here."

"What does she mean, 'bus stop'?" I asked Miranda, who was following behind now. I was expected to lead in front.

"That's it, that pole sticking out of the pavement," Miranda announced as we both sat down.

"We have to wait for a bus to come." Paddy looked at me. "The city's too far to walk. Here's one now. You go on first, Emma. Lead on."

I jumped on to the bus. It was much bigger than a car and much noisier, although I'd got used to most of the noises by now. There were rows and rows of seats. Lots of people sat there chattering away.

"What do we do now?" I asked Miranda. "Where do we go?"

"Well, we've got to find an empty seat. You'll have to learn to do that as you get a bit older." I looked around the bus. I couldn't see one anywhere.

Paddy walked forward. "Come on, Emma, down here. Here's an empty seat."

I followed her, and she sat down next to someone else.

"Under the seat, Miranda. You follow, Emma."

It was a bit of a squash under there with me and Miranda, and it was so dirty. The floor was filthy. There were all sorts of bits of paper on it. "I don't like these things," I said to Miranda. "They're not clean like the car, are they? Why is this floor so dirty, look at all the papers? Ugh, I've got something stuck to my paw."

"Here, I'll get it off for you," Miranda said, rather kindly I thought, so I gave her my paw. She licked it very delicately and got the piece of paper off. She didn't let go of the piece of paper, I noticed, but continued chewing it.

"What is it?" I said.

She suddenly spat it out. "Nothing. Nothing at all. They are sweet papers and they are not to be picked up."

"Oh!" I said, thinking . . . well, she picked it up and chewed it before she spat it out again. I daren't say anything to her because I knew she would get very annoyed. I started to look round with fresh interest. Yes, there was another one over there. I sniffed at it.

"Leave it!" Miranda said. "Don't get into bad habits. Leave them alone."

I found the city a fascinating place. The shops were so much bigger than in our town.

"Forward," Paddy said, as we walked along the pavement.

Forward? I thought. What does she mean.

"Lead on, Emma, in front."

"She wants you to walk in front of her," Miranda said.

She kept behind Paddy on the right hand side. I had to stay on the left.

"Oh, I see. Like this." I moved off.

"There's a clever girl," Paddy said. "We really have to get down to some serious training now, Emma. Sit at the kerbs and watch for the traffic. You must not go across the roads until it's quite clear. Forward," she said again. I got up to cross the road. "No Emma, there's a car coming. Look." And there was. But wasn't it Paddy's job to make sure that the road was clear before we crossed? And then I remembered what Sugar had told me about guide dogs. Of course I had to learn how to cross the road. I felt it was a big responsibility for me to make sure that Paddy and Miranda got across the road safely. Then I had another surprise. In a large shop, Paddy told me to find the lift. I hadn't any idea what she meant. I'm sure she didn't expect me to go straight to it, because every time Paddy asked me to find something she did show it to me first.

"Here it is," she said, pressing a button on the wall and, magically, some doors opened in front of us. In we went. It was a peculiar feeling in the lift—a sort of floating sensation. The doors opened again and out we got, but we were in a completely different place. It took me quite a long time before I realised what lifts were. They did the same as stairs but you didn't have to do any climbing. You just walked in and stood there and walked out again and you were on another floor. I quite liked that idea.

I can't say I particularly liked the station, the railway station that is, where we went next. They're such noisy places. In fact, when we went down the steps and along what they called the platform, the ground began to shudder beneath my feet and there was a terrible noise. I had to

71

flatten my ears back to my head to try and keep some of the sound out.

"Don't be afraid," Paddy said. She stroked my head. "It's only a train. You have to get used to them. We'll be going on one soon when we go on our holidays. When this one stops you can get in and have a look. It's like a bus really."

I wasn't very keen about getting into one of these. In fact, Miranda had to go first.

"Come on," she sneered, "there's nothing to be frightened of in here. If you don't get on the train you won't be able to go on your holiday and see the seaside."

I didn't want to miss out on that so I followed her in. There wasn't much in there, just seats like on a bus. There was nothing to be frightened of really—it was just that horrible noise they made when they came into the station.

There were so many things I saw that day in the city—the railway station, lifts, zebra crossings (they're the safest places to cross the road—a dog doesn't have to bother about traffic on those, you just have to sit there and eventually all the traffic will stop). My head was a whirl by the time I got home and I didn't even want to discuss things with Miranda when I got into bed, although she wanted to talk. She wanted to tell me all about the holiday that we were going on.

"The sea," she kept saying, "is so lovely. You'll want to swim in it all day."

"I don't think so," I said. "If I don't like puddles, I'm sure I won't like the sea."

"Oh you will. It's so totally different from puddles. It's much nicer. Anyway, there's always the sand. You can dig in that. You have to be extremely well behaved when we go on holiday. Hotels don't normally allow dogs in but, of course, we're special. You have to be very, very quiet. They don't allow barking in hotels."

But I couldn't stop awake any longer. I don't know whether she told me any more because I fell asleep.

Chapter 9

On Holiday

A few weeks later we were back at the railway station again. We were actually going on our holiday that Miranda had talked so much about. The train journey wasn't as bad as I'd expected it to be. It wasn't so noisy once you were inside. It was a peculiar sensation, not like a car or a bus—a sort of swaying movement, which sent me off to sleep most of the time.

"Come on, you silly dog, wake up. We're there!" Miranda was poking me with her nose. "Can't you smell the lovely sea air? Mmmm, it's beautiful."

We were off the train and out of the station and, sure enough, there was a different sort of smell. Exciting. A foody smell as well as a fresh tingle to the nose. There were far more food shops than there seemed to be at home, with smells of onions, and sausages, and something else that I later found out was candy-floss.

"Hush," Miranda said as we went in through the door of the hotel. "Now remember what I told you about dogs and hotels. Children and dogs are not allowed to run along the corridors, and no noise, either."

I crept behind her as we went up in a lift and Paddy took us into what was going to be our room for the next week.

"It's very nice," I whispered to Miranda. "The carpets are

lovely on the floor, aren't they, but where's our bed?"

"Paddy's got a blanket for us. We'll just have to sleep on the floor. It won't hurt you for a week, surely."

"No, I don't mind."

"You don't have to whisper. We're in our own room now. Nobody else will hear us."

"Oh good."

"Look, Paddy's putting the case down and we're obviously going straight out on to the beach."

I'd never seen Miranda pull on the lead before but she did on the way to the beach. As soon as we got there Paddy let us off.

"Off you go, you two. Go and have a play."

Miranda was gone in a flash to the sea. It was a huge expanse of water and it moved backwards and forwards. I didn't trust it at all.

"Come on," Miranda called as she disappeared into the distance, "it's marvellous out here."

"No thank you," I shouted back. "I don't like the look of that." I don't think she heard me. I couldn't see her any more, she had gone out of sight completely.

The sand was all right for a dig, but I soon got fed up making holes in it. "What shall I do?" I asked Paddy. Of course, she couldn't understand. She was sitting reading. Oh dear, I thought, am I going to have to spend the whole week on this beach and not have anything to do?

Luckily, Mandy turned up. Mandy was a little girl. Now there are children and children, and Mandy was a very nice child. There are so many of them who don't know how to treat dogs and they pulled my ears, or stood on my tail, or tried to mimic my barking, and so many children scream. There were quite a few children playing on the beach. I didn't like to go near them because they were rolling this way and that way and screaming. I hate to hear children scream. It goes right through my ears, makes them burn inside. I had to keep barking at them to tell them to be quiet but they didn't listen to me.

Well Mandy, as I say, was completely different. She came up to me and started stroking me and she had something on a stick that smelled delicious. I had a lick of it. Well . . . I mean . . . what's a dog supposed to do? She was waving it in front of my nose and it was very nice. Candy-floss, she called it. I did get it stuck round my nose and some of it on my ears. Miranda had a delightful time licking it off, I may tell you.

"What a lovely colour she is. What is she?" she asked Paddy.

"She's a labrador. A chocolate labrador, but you don't see many about."

"Oh, I have never seen one before. I'll go and tell my Mum and Dad. They'd love to see her." She ran off and I saw her Mum and Dad sitting down by the water's edge.

"That's a chocolate labrador," she called. "Come and have a look."

"Oh, we'll come a bit later. You go and talk to her," they called back.

"How old is she?" Mandy asked Paddy.

"She's about eleven months now. She's going to be a guide dog."

"How marvellous. We're saving for a guide dog at our

school. You know, we're collecting tin foil. It's very expensive to train a guide dog."

"It costs over two thousand pounds now," Paddy told her.

"You are beautiful, and obviously you're a clever dog. What's her name?"

"Emma."

"Aren't you big! I bet you eat a lot of meat a day."

"Yes she does," Paddy said. "So does Miranda."

"Who's Miranda?"

"She's another labrador. A yellow one, but she's gone off swimming," Paddy said, pointing in the direction in which Miranda had disappeared.

"I'd like to go out but my Mum and Dad won't let me. I brought my Li-lo today, though, so perhaps they will let me go out on that."

"Can you swim?" Paddy asked her.

"No, but I'm learning at school."

"Well, I don't think you ought to go into the sea, then."

"Your dog's gone into the sea."

"Yes, she can swim."

"Can Emma swim?"

"Well, I think so. But she doesn't seem to like the water."

"Never mind, Emma, you can stop with me. I've got a ball somewhere. We'll go and play with that."

If it hadn't been for Mandy and her candy-floss I would have been very bored, especially as the weather got hot and you couldn't dash around much. I suppose Miranda was right, it was much cooler in the sea, but I daren't risk it. Paddy wasn't much company either. All she seemed to want to do was to lie on the beach all day and sleep. Mandy's parents were always going to sleep, too, and she would come and talk to me—except when she was on her Li-lo. That was a rubber thing that floated in the sea and she used to sit on top of it and paddle about and her parents were always shouting at her not to go very far.

One afternoon they'd obviously gone to sleep again, because Mandy was on her Li-lo and had gone quite a distance from the shore. Oh well, if there was nothing else to do I'd have a nap as well.

No sooner had I shut my eyes than I heard Mandy screaming. "Oh, I wish she wouldn't do that. Can't a dog

have a nap in peace?" I sat up and had a look. She was a long way out and she was still screaming. "Don't make that noise," I shouted. "Oh, stop screaming," I barked. If only she'd stop, it was a horrible noise. I rushed down to the water's edge. "Stop it! Stop it! You're driving me mad." She wouldn't be quiet. I had to go and tell Paddy. "Can't you tell her to stop screaming?" I barked at Paddy.

"What's the matter, Emma? Go away and play somewhere, I want a bit of peace. What's that?" Paddy sat up. "Is that somebody screaming?"

"Yes," I barked. "Can't you hear her? Shout to her and tell her to shut up. She won't take any notice of me."

"Hey! What's Mandy doing right out there?" Paddy rushed over to Mandy's parents, started shaking them and shouting at them. All of a sudden there seemed to be chaos on the beach. Mandy's father raced into the sea and in no time at all he brought Mandy back and she was crying.

"I've told you not to go out to sea. You are a naughty girl. What would have happened if Emma hadn't started barking and woken us all up?"

Paddy looked round at me. "Emma, you saved Mandy's life. You are a clever dog."

Mandy's mother and father came over to look at me for the first time. They started to stroke me.

"You are a good girl, Emma. Mandy might have drowned if you hadn't woken us up."

Mandy came and put her arms round me. "Oh Emma! Oh, thank you, Emma. What can I get you? Can I bring her a packet of dog biscuits or a bone tomorrow, just to say thank you for saving my life?"

"You must never go out to sea again on that Li-lo," her father warned.

"Oh, I won't, Dad. Honest I won't."

In the middle of all this Miranda came back, wet through. She shook herself all over me. "What's all this fuss about? I heard a lot of shouting and screaming, I thought I'd better come and see what was happening."

I didn't realise I had saved Mandy's life, not until they told me. It was a good job I barked, I thought. I wouldn't let on to Miranda that I didn't know what I was doing. "Well, it was me. I saved Mandy's life."

"What do you mean, you saved Mandy's life?" She grinned at me.

"She was going to be drowned. If I hadn't barked she might well have been."

"Well, what happened?"

I told her the story in full, missing out, of course, that it was Mandy's screaming that made me bark because it upset me so much. I didn't say that I hadn't realised that she was going to drown—that would have spoilt the whole story. Well, Miranda didn't say much after that. She didn't even go swimming the rest of that day. She sat on the beach and watched. She did treat me with a bit more respect after that. In fact, I think Miranda had got quite attached to me. I didn't realise how much, though, until I was leaving for the Training Centre after we had come back from our holiday.

Chapter 10

In Harness

We were in the back of the car on the way to the Training Centre when I suddenly realised that I'd never see Miranda and Paddy again. I was going to be a guide dog.

"This is it!" Miranda announced. "You are actually going to the kennels."

"Oh Miranda! I know it's a very special job and I know I've been trained for it but I really don't want to go. I don't want to leave you and Paddy. Couldn't I stop with you all the time? Surely they could find plenty of dogs to be guide dogs. It's so nice being with you and Paddy."

"Now, don't be silly. You're a very intelligent dog. In fact, you'll probably make the best guide dog they've ever had, and there's somebody who can't see who's waiting for you. What are they going to do if you come back home with us?"

"Well, yes, I know, but it's so awful to think that I will never see you again. Couldn't I stay . . . please?"

"No, you must be a guide dog." She came across and started to lick my face. "Really, Emma, you will make a good guide dog. Mark my words, you'll forget all about me and Paddy soon. There will be so much work to do, lots of new friends and a blind person to look after."

It didn't make parting any easier, and when I got out of

the car and Paddy took me to a kennel maid, I daren't look back at Miranda. I was so upset. I didn't even say goodbye. I heard Paddy walking back to the car and I followed the kennel maid into the kennels. I felt so alone. I looked out of the window in the hope of seeing somebody in the run but there was no one there. "Oh Miranda!" I called. "Don't leave me!"

I don't know how long I cried for, it seemed hours to me. The only time I had ever been left on my own before was at Christmas, and I remembered tearing the Christmas tree up. That made me feel even more lonely. I wouldn't be spending another Christmas with Miranda.

The kennel maid came back. "Emma, what's all that noise about? Here you are, I've got a friend for you now. There's no need to cry any more. In you go, there's a good boy."

She closed the gate. I turned round to see a very large yellow labrador. He suddenly bounded towards me.

"Hi there, Emma. How are you?"

It was Anton. I hadn't recognised him at first, he'd grown so much.

"Oh, Anton. How lovely to see you."

"Was that you howling?" he asked.

"Yes, but I was so lonely, Anton, and I didn't think anyone was going to come, ever, and it was so terrible to say goodbye to Miranda and Paddy and I'm never going to see them again."

"Yes, I hate goodbyes," he admitted, sitting on the bed next to me, "but still, we have got so much to look forward to. Now, tell me, Emma, what have you been doing these last few months? How much more have you learned about being a guide dog? And how is Miranda?"

I told him how I had been all around the shops and the city and about saving Mandy's life at the seaside—but I told Anton the truth.

"I bet you didn't tell Miranda that you didn't realise what was happening," he said with a smile.

"I didn't."

"Did she have a bit more respect for you after that, then?"

"Yes, I think she did. In fact, to be absolutely honest with you, I'm sure she was sad I was leaving home. She just wouldn't admit it."

The kennel maid went past several times that day and two more dogs settled into nearby kennels—a black labrador with a very shiny coat called Josephine, and another yellow labrador, Cindy. Later that evening when we all met up in the run we were joined by a black labrador called Arrow. I must confess, I didn't like him right from the beginning. It was the way he rebuffed us all when he first came in.

"Hi!" Anton called as he saw him coming through the gate. "My name's Anton. This is Emma, Josephine and Cindy." He pointed his nose at each of us, introducing us.

"Huh," Arrow said, and ignored us.

"Where are you from?" I asked him.

"Warwick."

"I've never heard of that place. Is it far away?"

"No."

He wasn't at all talkative and, as hard as we all tried to bring him into the conversation, we just couldn't get anything out of him at all. The rest of us were so excited about being guide dogs and what it would mean to us, but Arrow never said a word.

The next morning our trainer came, Mr Peel. He was going to take each of us out individually. I was lucky, I went first.

"Hello, Emma. You're a nice little chocolate labrador. Well, let's see how much you know, shall we?"

He put on my collar and lead. I was a bit surprised, and looked round for the harness I'd heard about. Perhaps he thought I wasn't going to be good enough to be a guide dog? I needn't have worried, though, because I found out later that all trainee guide dogs stay on a lead for about three weeks before they have to wear a harness—and even then the trainer uses the lead. It's not until you're really good that the trainer uses the harness as a blind person would.

We went out of the Training Centre and along the main road. The smells out there were wonderful. Hundreds of dogs must have passed. Humans don't realise how tantalising the smells are and I just couldn't help stopping to sniff.

"No, Emma. Leave. When you're on duty you mustn't stop and sniff."

I'd forgotten for a moment. Paddy had told me many times.

"When you're not guiding you can do as you please and stop and sniff, but at the moment you work." He emphasised the word work.

I kept twitching my nose. I could still smell the odours drifting past, but I resisted the urge to investigate.

"You must sit at the kerb, Emma, and make sure that the road is clear."

I knew that and sat down straight away.

"You have to look right and then left." He pointed each way with his hand. "There's nothing coming now. Forward, Emma."

Off I went in front of him.

"You're a clever dog. You know what that means. We'll go into town and see what you think of all the people and the traffic."

Of course, I was so used to going into the town, pneumatic drills and big lorries never bothered me any more. Mr Peel was very pleased. He made a big fuss of me before I went back into the kennel. It was Anton's turn to go out next.

We didn't see Mr Peel again that day. In the afternoon we were all let out into a grass paddock so we could have lots of time to play and chase each other around.

"Isn't this great!" Anton called across the paddock. "This is a lovely life."

"We shall have to start work soon though," Cindy reminded him.

Arrow, who seemed to be busying himself in a corner sniffing some long grass, looked up at Cindy's comment. "Huh! Don't know about that. Don't like the thought of this sort of work at all."

I was amazed. What did he mean? "Don't you want to be a guide dog?" I asked him in astonishment.

"No, not at all. Horrible."

"I can't understand you. You mean you really don't want to be one?"

"I've just said so, haven't I? No. What more do you

want?" He turned his back on me and never said another word to any of us that day.

After tea that evening we all slept peacefully. I was tired out after my outing with Mr Peel and playing in the paddock all afternoon, and there was work to do tomorrow.

For the next few weeks Mr Peel took me out every day, and we went over and over the things Paddy and Miranda had taught me until I understood exactly what to do.

During this time we were moved to a different block of kennels. I found out from other dogs I met that we'd been in special kennels to get used to the Training Centre—it was so different from the homes we'd been puppy-walked in—but now we were in the main block,. where all the adult dogs lived. It was lovely—we were all put in the same big kennel, me and Anton, Cindy and Josephine . . . and Arrow, worst luck. He was so unfriendly!

One morning, Mr Peel had a white harness with him. He put it on my back, though it didn't have the handle on it.

"There we are, Emma. You just get used to wearing that harness before I use the handle. Well, you don't seem to mind it at all."

Apparently some dogs hate the harness, the feel of leather around their back and under their tummy and chest, but it didn't bother me—probably because I knew what it was for.

I led the way out of the Training Centre, remembering not to put my nose to the ground.

"I think I'll teach you how to walk round people today, Emma. You see, if you're guiding a blind person, whenever you walk round an obstacle or a person, you must make sure that they don't walk into anything. Here are some people coming along now."

I walked straight towards them but Mr Peel guided me over to the right so that I passed them and he had plenty of room to walk by the side of me.

"That's it, Emma. Now then, let's see if we can find another obstacle. Ah, somebody's left a pram outside the shop."

This time he couldn't take me to the right as the pram was sticking out onto the pavement, so he started to go left.

"Left, Emma. Go round it. That's it. There's a good girl."

This was easy, I thought. I just had to keep taking him round things that we came across on the pavement, sitting at the kerbs, crossing each road. Until, at the next kerb, he gave me the command to turn right. "What does that mean?" I looked up at him. He was pointing his hand down the road.

"Right, Emma." He stepped back and guided me with the lead. "That's it, that's right. Once you've learnt that, I can show you how to turn left and back. You seem to know forward quite well."

It must have been about a week before I actually got the white handle on the harness so that I could guide properly. That was a funny feeling. Mr Peel walked behind me holding the lead and the handle and I was learning to guide by walking the same distance in front of him all the time. I was practising what left and right and back meant and I was beginning to get the idea of how to take him round things on the pavement. It was so easy to misjudge. I'd think there was plenty of room for him then I'd hear him knock into something. I'd look round to see him behind me all mixed up with some people, or I'd led him into a pram or a bike on the pavement. That was awful. He could see, I knew that, but what if I did that to someone who couldn't? He never got annoyed with me. He always took me back and showed me how to walk round the obstacle correctly and then gave me lots of praise. It was lovely working with him. I really enjoyed it.

I had to learn how to go up and down steps. There were lots of steps all over the place. I was surprised, I'd never really noticed them before—apart from kerbs, where I just had to sit when we went down the step, and it didn't matter about going up the step on the other side because I was in

front. Going up and down flights of steps was a different matter. There was a flight of steps in the Training Centre just outside the kennels, so we were able to practise there. I had to sit at the top and then when I was told to go foward, to gently step onto the very first step and wait until I could see that Mr Peel had got his foot down, and then gently step onto the next step and so on until we got to the bottom. Going up a flight of steps I also had to sit down and, again, go very gently up the steps, watching to make sure that Mr Peel had got to the step behind me before I moved up again. As I always seemed to be the one to go out first, every time I got back to the kennel they all wanted to know what I'd been doing—except Arrow that is, who did nothing but sit on the bed and mope.

"Where have you been this morning?" Anton said, almost before I'd got in the gate.

"We've been going up and down steps, just outside the kennels."

"What do we have to do?" Josephine asked.

"Oh, I'm sure Mr Peel will tell you much better than I can. Don't forget, though, that you mustn't sniff. There are some delicious smells at the top of those steps. I think the kitchen's off there, where they prepare the dog meat."

"Yes, it is," Anton confirmed. "I smelt it when I passed yesterday. So we have to go up and down those steps, do we?"

"Yes. You must sit at the top and you must sit at the bottom and go very carefully." Cindy, Josephine and Anton always listened with great interest to what I had to say, what I'd been doing and where we were all hoping to go next. Arrow took no notice at all. I was never able to understand his hatred for the thought of being a guide dog. I was always longing to go out and after my first turn in the morning, I couldn't wait for the others to come back and tell me what they'd been doing. I looked forward with longing to the afternoon, when I could go out with Mr Peel again.

Next came letter-boxes and telephone boxes. I was walking down the main road when, suddenly, Mr Peel stopped and asked me to look for a telephone box. "What in the world is one of those?" He obviously didn't understand what I was asking him but he must have realised I didn't know.

"There's a telephone box, Emma. Over there." He pointed to a tall, red thing with windows in it. I'd always wondered what they were for.

"Off you go, Emma, to the telephone box." He guided me towards it. I sat down immediately I got there. "You must find the door now, Emma. Find the door."

What did he mean "find the door"? I couldn't see a door anywhere. It was all glass windows. He took me round the box and pointed at a catch on one side, then he pulled the door open. I'd never have guessed that was a door. How marvellous. You could go in these things. It was very difficult to find the door. I'd have to be very careful I took my owner to the right side of the box.

Then we went on to letter-boxes and, again, they were rather funny things—red and tall but completely different from telephone boxes, with no windows, and I had to stop at the side where the slit was at the top. I'd often need to walk right round before I noticed it.

It was when I was telling Cindy and Anton about the things I'd seen with Mr Peel—telephone boxes and letter-boxes—that the noise began. There was a terrible barking and snarling, people shouting, and we all rushed to the window. I thought I could see Arrow at the top of the run and Mr Peel and a couple of kennel maids.

"What's happening?" Anton said, as he put his nose out of the window.

"Don't know. Something's going on up there. Is that Arrow?"

"Yes, looks like it. Goodness me, there's another dog there as well."

I wasn't big enough to see right out of the window. "Well, what are they doing?"

"Don't know," said Anton. "Looks like a dog fight to me."

"A dog fight!" I was horrified. I'd never been involved in one myself, though I'd heard about them from Miranda.

Then we heard Mr Peel coming down the corridor. "You bad dog, Arrow. You'll never make a guide dog if you fight. I've got my doubts whether you've got the ability to guide a blind person." The gate opened and Arrow came in. Mr Peel slammed the gate and I heard his footsteps going back down the corridor. I daren't ask Arrow what happened, he looked so mad, but Anton did.

"What was all that about then?"

Arrow growled from the bed.

"Well, come on. We've got a right to know; you're sharing our kennel."

I'd never heard Anton be so authoritative.

Arrow growled again. "Nasty dogs. Hateful people. I don't want to be a guide dog."

"You've obviously had fight with someone." Anton got closer and bared his teeth at him. "I'm the top dog of this kennel and you do as I tell you. No dog fights in my kennel."

Arrow snarled. I was frightened. In fact, Cindy, Josephine and I went off to the furthest corner.

"Oh, don't fight!" Josephine called. "Please don't fight! You heard what Mr Peel said."

Anton started to back off. "Huh, he's not worth fighting with." And he turned his back on Arrow and came to sit with us.

It was only later that we heard what had happened. A lovely little golden retriever had been passing the kennels when suddenly Arrow leapt out at her and grabbed her ear for no reason at all. The poor little soul was so shaken she wasn't able to do any more training that day.

That night, when Arrow was asleep, Anton confided in me.

"He definitely won't make a guide dog if he's going to be like that. Can you imagine what people would think if dogs like him were wearing white harnesses and responsible for blind people? I wouldn't like anybody to say that about us, would you, that we're nasty I mean, and that's the sort of reputation he'd get us guide dogs."

It just made me all the more determined to be a guide dog, and I tried to remember everything Miranda had told me—and, of course, I'd never fight with another dog.

Chapter 11

Meeting Sheila

The months flew by. My days were so full of learning new things that I almost forgot I'd be meeting a new person soon. A blind person. Anton reminded me one evening after we'd had our tea.

"I've seen them come," he said. "I wonder when we're going to meet them?"

"Who? Who have you seen come?"

"Our new owners, of course. The blind people who we are going to look after."

"I'd almost forgotten," I admitted to him. "When did they come? What did they look like?"

"Well, I didn't get a chance to see," he said. "They came this afternoon when you were out. I knew it was them, they were all carrying suitcases. There were two women and two men. I expect I'll have a man."

"Why?"

"I'm a big dog so I need a tall person. You will probably have a woman because you're so small."

"I don't think I mind," I told him. Cindy and Josephine didn't seem to mind who they got. As long as it was someone nice.

"I've been told they are all nice, otherwise they wouldn't

have a guide dog," Josephine assured me. "They have to be trained as well, you know."

"What do you mean?" I asked. "People, human beings, they don't need to be trained. Only dogs are trained, surely."

"Oh no. A blind person must come here for a whole month, not only for us to get used to them but for them to learn how to look after us and how to work with us and how to give us the right commands."

"I never thought of that," Anton said, sitting back. "Fancy people being trained."

When everyone had settled down that evening, Anton crept over to me and whispered in my ear. "Only four people came," he said.

"Yes."

"Well, there are five dogs. Don't you see?"

I must have looked very mystified.

"One of us isn't going to be a guide dog," he went on. "It means that one of us has failed."

I was suddenly stricken with horror. "What do you mean, failed?" I said.

"Every dog doesn't make a guide dog, you know. I mean, we're not all clever enough."

I could feel my heart pounding in my ears with terror. Was it me? Was it me who wasn't good enough to be a guide dog? What had I done wrong? Mr Peel had always said how clever I was. "Oh . . . Anton! Oh, if it's me I don't know what I shall do. I so want to be a guide dog."

"It isn't you, you silly girl. It's him over there."

I looked across to where Anton was pointing his nose, to

the big black labrador still claiming most of the bed.

"Arrow! Hasn't he made it?"

"No. I heard the trainer telling the kennel maid today. He's going tomorrow."

"Going where?" I hardly dared ask.

"Oh, nothing horrible," he assured me. "The dogs that don't make guide dogs go out to be pets. You know, just live with families, to be ordinary dogs."

"I wouldn't like that."

"No, neither would I." Anton sat back thoughtfully. "Mind you, I must admit, I didn't think he was guide dog material. Did you, Emma?"

"Well, I've never got on very well with him. Have you?"

"Wouldn't speak. Wouldn't tell me where he came from. Wouldn't tell me anything about whether he'd been puppy-walked or just found in the street one day. Although, of course, they don't pick dogs up from the street to be guide dogs, do they, but . . . well, I mean, he was always complaining. Didn't like the white harness, didn't like the traffic in town, didn't like the thought of having to take a blind person about for the rest of his life. He's not the sort of dog we want to represent us, now is he?"

"No, I must admit you're right there, Anton, but I feel very sorry."

"Huh, don't feel sorry for him, he's absolutely delighted. All he wants to do is laze about all day and do nothing in particular. I've no time for a dog like him, no time at all. No, don't you worry, Emma. You're going to be a guide dog and I'm going to be a guide dog too."

Mr Peel was late the next morning so we all knew some-thing different was going to happen. When he did come he seemed to be excited.

"Well now, who shall we take first? Anton, I think. You come along and meet your new owner."

Off he went with Anton. It seemed ages before he came back again, and then it was my turn.

"Come along, Emma. Come on into the house."

We went into the big house. I had never been in there before, we had always stayed in the kennels. Up some stairs and along a corridor, then he opened a door.

"This is your dog. Her name's Emma. Off you go, Emma, and make friends. I'll see you later, Sheila, when you've got to know each other."

He closed the door behind him and I stood there, not quite knowing what to do. Sheila, who was sitting on the bed on the other side of the room, started to clap her hands and call my name. I couldn't help rushing towards her, putting my paws on her, licking her face.

"Hello, Emma. Aren't you beautiful?" She started to feel my coat. "Stay still a moment so I can feel you."

I couldn't. I was so excited, I wanted to dash about the room. She seemed so nice. What could I give her? Ah . . . some shoes over there. I picked one up and gave it to her.

"That's kind of you, Emma. Thank you. But just keep still a moment while I feel what you're like."

I sat down between her feet. She felt my face and my ears, along my body, my tail, my paws. She felt everywhere. It was so strange to think that she couldn't see me so she had to feel all over me.

"You do feel a nice dog, Emma. I hope we're going to get on well together."

"I'm sure we are," I told her, pushing my nose into her hand to reassure her. "I've been looking forward to meeting you." I knew she couldn't understand me but I had to say something.

That very afternoon I took Sheila for her first walk. Mr Peel came with me, of course. He stood right beside me while Sheila put the harness on.

"This white handle that Emma guides you with is very sensitive and you must hold it correctly, otherwise it will be uncomfortable for Emma and you won't be able to interpret what she does."

I looked round and watched Mr Peel placing Sheila's hand on the handle, but it all seemed so natural to me. I never thought about how Mr Peel held the handle or how he walked behind me, but I realised the difference when Sheila began to grip.

"No, don't hold the handle like that. That will make Emma feel stiff and uneasy. You must hold it very lightly, just hold your fingers around it gently so that it can move in your hand and then you will find that you're moving correctly with Emma. You must be very quick to respond to Emma's actions and you can only do that if you concentrate on the feeling from the handle and from Emma. I'll give her the commands," he told her, "and you just follow behind. It's very difficult for her. She's been used to me, so you must give her time to get used to you. Forward, Emma."

I was determined to show Sheila how clever I was so I leapt up and trotted at my fastest speed down the road.

"Oh. . . . Emma! Don't go so fast!" she called.

I could hear her behind me. She seemed to be running and stopping and falling over her feet. I slowed down a little. Didn't she want me to go fast? What was the matter with her?

"I can't keep this pace up," I could hear her panting.

"You'll be all right," Mr Peel assured her. "Guide dogs are trained to walk fast. You don't want to dawdle along the pavement, do you? You'll get used to it."

A kerb came and I stopped and sat down. She didn't. She fell down the kerb in front of me. "What are you doing?" I said to her. Mr Peel started laughing.

"You must stop when Emma stops," he said, and helped her back to the right position behind me.

"I don't know if I will ever get used to this. I feel as if I'm being dragged along behind a racing car," Sheila said.

Mr Peel laughed again. "You want your freedom, so you'll have to learn how to use your dog. Now then, you must listen for traffic and Emma will look."

She appeared to be listening. I could see there was nothing coming and I was longing to set off again.

"Forward," Mr Peel commanded me, and off I went. Sheila seemed to get a bit better as we went along. She wasn't stumbling so much. I could understand why the blind people had to come and spend a month. They certainly did need some training on how to use us dogs.

It was lovely to be in the house, and I had Sheila all to myself. I shared her room with her. There was a big bed in the corner for me and I went down to the canteen when Sheila had her meals. I was told to sit quietly under the table but, of course, I had learnt how to do that in Mavis's cafe. Nothing would make me move from under a table when somebody was eating. I missed the company of dogs at night when I got into my bed. I felt so lonely. There had always been a dog to talk to. I know I had Sheila but, of course, she couldn't understand what I was saying. Still I often met the other dogs in the lounge in the evenings and Anton and I could tell each other how we were getting on.

"Harry's extremely good but then he's had guide dogs before so he knows all about it."

"Oh, Sheila hasn't," I admitted. "She was a bit awful at first, kept falling over me, fell over the first kerb."

Anton laughed. "She'll be all right soon."

"I'm sure she will. She was a lot better this morning."

We would sit and listen to the human conversation and then discuss it ourselves. I heard Sheila telling Harry that she had rung her workmates and told them all about me.

"What does she mean?" I said to Anton. "Workmates?"

"They're her friends where she works."

"Does that mean she actually goes out to work?" I asked him.

"Yes, of course. They all do."

"How can they work if they can't see?"

"There's a girl here who can't see and she works. Haven't you noticed her?"

"No," I admitted. "Where?"

"In the reception. She's on the telephone. Carol, I think they call her. Haven't you noticed her dog, a black labrador, curled up?"

"Oh yes, I have. I never realised Carol couldn't see,

though, because she was working so well—all those plugs and switches and wires."

"That's right," Anton said. "She's a telephonist. Her dog was telling me the other day. I stopped to have a natter with her when I passed. A lot of blind people are telephonists. It's something that they can do really well, apparently."

"How do they read things? I mean, I've never seen them pick up books and papers. Not like Paddy used to."

"They have something called Braille. It's very strange. If you look about some evenings you'll perhaps see it on the tables. It's not like ordinary paper, it's brown and it's got little dots on. I ran my nose along it once and it tingled."

"Oh yes, I've seen lots of that about," I told him. "Braille. But how do they see it?"

"They don't see it." Anton laughed. "They feel it with their fingers. You watch, I bet Sheila will pick up something tonight and read it."

Sure enough, she did. Later on she picked one of those big brown paper things up and started to feel it with her fingers. How fascinating, I thought. I don't think I could do that with my paws. Mind you, I can't read anyway, but what's the point when you're a dog?

Chapter 12

Going Home

Sheila had to learn all the things that I'd already been taught, like how to cross the road at a zebra crossing. When she wanted to use a zebra crossing she had to put one foot onto the road to indicate to the motorist that she was going to cross, wait until she heard a car stop, and then give me the command to go. I liked zebra crossings. They were so easy. I'd always take her to one if I could see one. She had to learn about telephone boxes, too. I'd take her to them, of course, but she had to feel for the little handle to get in with. In shops I would take her up to the counter; all she had to do was ask for what she wanted and tell me to find the door again.

She was absolutely amazed at how I could take her round all the people in the town. We'd go shopping some days and it would be really busy. I loved getting through all the people. I'd see them coming towards me and decide whether I would take Sheila left or right. I'd rush round them so quickly, she was amazed.

"I have never got round town so fast," she admitted to Mr Peel one afternoon. "Isn't it lovely? All those crowds and I never walked into any of them."

Of course, what she didn't realise was that although I had to work and take her round people, most of the time they realised I was a guide dog—they saw the white harness—so they would step aside and let me through. I soon found that wearing the white harness was like magic because all the people in the streets respected me, but there was a lot of misunderstanding. They didn't realise how well I was trained, or that Sheila and I were taught to work together as a team.

I think I've already told you how the handle must be held with a guide dog—very lightly so that I could feel what Sheila was doing and she could feel what I was doing—and it was quite distressing to me when people stopped me, wanting to help. They'd grab hold of the handle and wrench it from Sheila's hand. Sometimes I'd feel as if I'd been swept off my feet. Of course, I knew they only wanted to help so I never complained and I realised Sheila tried to keep her temper too, thanking people but explaining that she must hold the handle. It's amazing how humans don't really listen to each other. Have you noticed? One day it happened, a lady grabbed the handle straight out of Sheila's hand.

"I'll help you," she called. "I'll take you across the road."

When I say "she called", I really mean she shouted. So many people seemed to shout at Sheila. I don't know why. Well, she did tell me, in the strictest confidence, that a lot of people who can see think those who are blind are also deaf. That's a laugh, she's got marvellous hearing! Anyway, as I was telling you, this lady shouted at us.

"I'm fine," Sheila said. "Thank you very much. We're just going along here. . ."

"Oh no, my dear, you must go across this road. I'll see

you across. Now don't worry about it."

Sheila tried to tell her that she didn't really want to cross the road, although it was very kind of her to stop and ask, but she wouldn't listen. She started to pull me, the lead and Sheila all at once across this busy main road and when we got to the other side, off she went and left us there. I sat down on the kerb and watched her disappearing into the crowd. Then I looked at Sheila.

"Oh dear, Emma. I'm sorry, you'll have to take me back across the road. We didn't want to come this way at all, did we?"

Human beings! There's nothing like them, is there?

I loved the daytimes. We were so busy, going out to different places, with Sheila always telling me what a clever dog I was. But I didn't like the nights. I got lonely, sleeping in my bed all on my own. So, one night when I was miserable and just couldn't stand it anymore, I got out of my bed and climbed onto Sheila's bed. I knew I was forbidden to do that—Sheila had told me—but she was fast asleep so she would never know until she woke up in the morning. It was so lovely to feel her warmth under the bedclothes and I didn't take up much room.

"I don't want to go to the railway station," I heard Sheila telling Mr Peel one morning. "I hate railway stations. I never want to go in one."

"You don't know that," Mr Peel told her. "Maybe you'll have to go on a train one day and there will be nobody to take you, so you've got to learn now. Trust Emma."

"Oh, but I'd much rather not. Please take the others and I'll stop in."

"No, you're not stopping in," Mr Peel said firmly, "you're going to the railway station and you can go first. You must trust Emma. She'll look after you."

I didn't know what all this fuss about railway stations was. When we got there, Mr Peel told her that I would take her in and to wait for him once we got to the platform. I knew she was nervous. I could feel it through the harness. It's amazing how much a dog can feel through the handle, exactly what her person is doing, even without looking round to see. I took her down the steps. I was very careful, knowing that she was scared. I walked along the platform and as soon as I got near the edge of the drop to the railway lines, I stopped and sat down. I looked round to see if Mr Peel was coming. There he was walking up the platform.

"There you are. So far, so good," he told Sheila. "Now, you're right at the edge of the platform. There's a drop in front of you to the railway lines. Tell Emma to go forward."

"I am not doing that," she shouted. "Oh no!"

"Don't be silly," Mr Peel told her. "You have got a highly trained guide dog there, you must trust her. Now tell her to go forward."

What was all the fuss about? Goodness me, didn't she trust me at all? I sat there waiting for her to tell me. I could hardly hear her whisper the word "Forward" but immediately she did I got up, turned my body in front of hers and pushed her back onto the platform where it was safe. She knelt down and put her arms around me.

"Oh, Emma, you are a clever dog. I'm so sorry, I didn't mean not to trust you."

"I should think not, indeed;" I told her as I licked her

face. "You can always trust me and I promise I'll look after you."

Anton chuckled that evening in the lounge when I told him about the railway station.

"Goodness me. Did she really think you'd jump over onto those lines?"

"I don't know," I told him.

"Well, really. As if us dogs could be so stupid. Of course, Harry did it but he knew what we'd do. If humans ever say 'forward' and there's danger in front of them, he knew we'd push them back. She'll soon get used to it all, Emma. Don't worry about it."

"I'm sure she will, but I wonder what'll happen when we go home. It's tomorrow, isn't it, and there'll be no Mr Peel to help us."

"You mustn't worry about that, Emma. They wouldn't dream of letting you and Sheila go off together to start a new way of life unless they knew you were both absolutely capable. Remember, you're a fully trained guide dog, you've passed all your tests and now Sheila is fully-trained too."

"What will it be like?" I asked him. "When we get home, I mean. Do you know?"

"Well, I've heard bits and bobs, you know, from various dogs. I think it's very nice. Of course, we're the family pet as well as the guide dog and you go out to work every day, so you make lots of new friends."

"Dog friends, do you mean?" I asked him in excitement.

"I don't know about dog friends, but you will make lots of new human friends. I suppose we will make other dog

friends. After all, we work so we have to play, remember. Mr Peel has told all the guide dog owners we have got to have free exercise every day, and I heard Sheila telling Harry there were some nice parks near where she worked and it would be lovely at dinner time to go out for a walk with you. I bet you'll meet lots of dogs."

"Yes, I suppose I will. Not many guide dogs though, Anton. It's so sad, I won't have anybody to discuss what's happened during the day with."

"You'll get used to it." He nuzzled one of my ears in reassurance. "You'll love being a guide dog. You won't want to discuss it with anyone. You'll be so confident in yourself, you'll know exactly what to do and where to take Sheila. Harry was talking the other night about his old guide dog, how he used to take him to work every day without him saying a word and how, in the evenings, he would take him out to friends, and all this sort of thing. Apparently, he just got to know exactly where Harry wanted to go. Well, we'll get like that, especially if we're careful and listen and remember all the things that we're told."

I was saying goodbyes to Anton and Cindy and Josephine. It was time for us to go. Sheila was taking me to her home, a place in Nottingham, she told me. "A house with a little garden, and we'll go out to work every day," she said. "You'll love that. You'll meet lots of people and they're all dying to see you at work."

"I don't suppose we'll ever meet again," Anton said. We were standing at the bus station, each of us catching different buses to our new homes. "Best of luck, Emma. I'm sure you're going to be a terrific guide dog."

I thanked him and assured him he already was. "And Harry's such a nice person," I told him.

"Well, Sheila is too. I think we're very lucky dogs to have such nice people. Don't you?"

110

"Come on, Emma," Sheila called.

The bus was coming in. "Bye, Anton."

"Bye, Emma."

It was strange to sit on the bus for such a long journey, to a new home I knew nothing about, to a new life I was so looking forward to. This was it. At last I was a fully trained guide dog, responsible for a blind person. I had to look after her whatever and wherever we went. We'd always be together.